The KINDER CHRONICLES

Big Life Lessons from Tiny Plastic Chairs

Vanessa Hardaway
and Gary L. Riggins

Dedication

This book is dedicated to the hard-working teachers who show up every day *in loco parentis, curantis, magister, nutrix, legatus, trapezitam, consilium*, etc. For those without a Latin dictionary handy, "in place of parents, babysitter, teacher, nurse, police officer, banker, counselor, etc."

Gary Riggins and Vanessa Hardaway

CONTENTS

Acknowledgments

We thank the many friends and family and a bunch of students who made this book possible. We need to thank Jodi Riggins, Janice, and Vant Hardaway for their patience and willingness to hear us out when sentences got stuck somewhere between our heads and the keyboard. Sure, they're family, but their kindness was more than an obligatory commitment. Their continuing examples of Christian charity in its many forms were deeply appreciated and helped make us and this book so much better. "Thank you" are just two little words that are so inadequate. We are grateful to have you in our lives.

We thank Drs. Jo Higginbotham, Delia Price, George Nerren, and Jason DeHart for the unenviable task of reading some of the rough early versions. Their encouragement and suggestions smoothed some of the rough edges and made what you will read much better. We are genuinely honored by their friendship. Thank you!

Another list of helpful suggestions and many "way to gos!" came from Evelyn McCray, Natalie Smith, Frenise Mann, Carole Haynes, and William O'Kelly. We are so moved by their generosity of spirit! Their help and suggestions in reading later drafts and just being there made a difference. They did what real friends do. They told the truth, and their kind words, comments, and corrections were instrumental in improving what you are about to read.

We thank our thousands of students over our combined sixty-five years in the teaching and learning business. Kids from kindergarten through graduate school have shared their lives and genuinely human stories with us. What we have learned from them is the foundation for this labor of love. Although we've not always been eager students, we proudly acknowledge the life lessons they've taught us. This book is a testament to what we've learned. Thanks so much!

Lastly and most importantly, we acknowledge the unseen hand of our Creator in the center of all of this. As simple instruments of God's peace, we've done what we believe we *had* to do, "write the vision and make it plain..." (Habakkuk 2:2). As another old writer put it, from here, we can only trust the mystery. What happens now—like this book—is in your hands.

Peace and Joy,

Gary L. Riggins

Vanessa Hardaway

Preface

A merry heart doeth good like a medicine...

Proverbs 17:22

Kids are funny, and so is Vanessa Hardaway. Thankfully for so many parents and children in and around Fayetteville, North Carolina, she happens to be a kindergarten teacher. Her encounters with her "snaggletooth babies" are an endless source of her material and the inspiration for this book. It grew out of a brief diary of observations and reflections of daily classroom life over forty days in a school year that she shared on *Facebook*.

After nearly two decades in the business of helping kids learn to distinguish "bs" and "ds," tie their shoes, and understand the consequences of fundamental bathroom etiquette, Vanessa recognized that life lessons were hiding in her notes if she looked close enough. Teaching and learning, especially at the kindergarten level, are two-way streets. Some of the things kindergarteners *taught her* were inspirational, and others were whimsical. In each story, she found a lesson on how to "do life." Vanessa's warm and infectious humor makes these lessons so inviting and easy to hear. Based on the positive response to her *Kinder*

Chronicles, I suggested she turn these insightful, hilarious, and tender reflections and the lessons they taught into a book. So here we are.

First, let me introduce my coauthor. I met Vanessa when she enrolled in a Graduate Program in Education that I directed at our university. She had a business degree, some banking experience, and a brief stint as a youth probation officer; however, she really wanted to retool and become a teacher. Her parents and several family members were all highly respected educators. It seemed fitting that she follow them into "the family business." She quickly became a class favorite of my colleagues and enjoyed the respect and friendship of her cohort. It was always a better (at least livelier) class if Vanessa was in it.

When she completed the program, she was chosen to speak for the graduates at the Commencement service, and true to form, she wowed the crowd. Her fifteen minutes in the spotlight remains one of the most quoted and cited student speeches in our history. The next day at graduation, our normally staid and stolid graduation speaker warmed up his audience with a quote from Vanessa's speech the night before that instantly won him their attention, sustained applause, and a lot of laughter. The audience was now ready to listen. Good teachers and preachers instinctively know that "a merry heart" is great medicine for even the most hard-hearted and psychosclerotic among us.

Since then, with her characteristic wit and wisdom, Vanessa has entertained and educated various audiences: her kindergarteners, my Educational Psychology classes, and a range of teacher and community workshops and seminars. I have had several guest lecturers in my undergraduate classes and heard many other speakers. She is my students' favorite speaker and, of course, mine.

She connects with those on the other side of the podium with a refreshing honesty that resonates with kids, pre-service teachers, and weary educators bogged down in too many unrealistic expectations. Her courage to laugh at the crazy absurdities in the human experience (especially in the classroom) reminds us of all the things that matter and unite us. We are messy people, all of us. Her message is inviting and affirming, and the warmth of her humor makes it so easy to hear. Unfortunately, not enough emotionally drained teachers have heard it.

Our profession is sick. According to a recent national Gallop Poll in Education (*Frustrations in the Schools*, *PDK*, September 2019), at least half of our teachers are fed up and looking for an exit. We simply can't afford this brain drain. This book attempts to stem that tide and bottle Vanessa's vibrant essence and share it with colleagues, some of whom are at their wit's end and simply need a good laugh. Her no-holds-barred retelling of what happened in her class—warts and all—

and the lessons she learned in those experiences may be just the medicine desperate, hard-working teachers need.

The truth is that the work of teaching and learning is challenging. It's also true that this work is done by imperfect, messy human beings on both sides of the teacher's desk. If you look hard enough, there's usually something to learn in our stories. But in our *Snapchat* society, we are typically too impatient to find it. However, for those who put in the work, the payoff is usually a scrap of ironic humor somewhere around the margins, making the lesson more palatable and more likely to stick.

Vanessa and I have tried to be faithful to the events that happened in her classroom. Though the names are changed, the kids are real, and their stories are *mostly* true (some settings were changed to protect their anonymity). As it turns out, smart-alec kindergarteners, the Lord, and even arrogant supervisors have a lot to teach. These lessons are sometimes painful and funny, but they are not always obvious. They tend to hide in plain sight, cleverly disguised in common experience. The title is our best guess at what the universe was trying to get across. Consequently, you can read Vanessa's experiences and be entertained without the hassle of trying to find Waldo. Spoiler alert, he's at the top of the page.

Most importantly, Vanessa and I encourage you to use this model and "cowboy up." Pay attention to your own stories, especially the "no fun" ones, but don't leave out what you could or should have learned in the process. If E.L. Thorndike was right, we learn everything in a trial-and-error process that can be embarrassing, sometimes distressing, but often hilarious. In these errors, we hone our skills in cooking, playing the piano, solving math problems, and especially teaching. However, it takes courage to admit that you have perhaps messed up. Without some reflection, errors are just painful failures.

Experiences are excellent teachers, but don't let your experiences bully you. Staring them down requires a lot of guts. There's an effective remedy for these occasional and inevitable discomforts in the teaching and learning process. Take the advice of a hilarious veteran teacher and an old professor...be more joyful along the way. To paraphrase an even older writer, "laughter is good medicine." Vanessa, her students, and I can testify. Finding joy—especially in the face of the most difficult of circumstances—will soothe your wounds, cure what ails you, and make learning much more fun.

Gary L. Riggins

August 25

There's Only One First Day

You're off to great places. Today is your first day! Your mountain is waiting, so get on your way!

Dr. Seuss

Today is special. The smell of fresh paint, new construction paper, white paste, and the satisfying assurance that every station is fully equipped are all strong evidence of a brand-spanking-new, fresh-out-of-the-box year. Of course, the new school year begins with a new day. Today I get to meet a new bunch of little people that will be in my care for a whole school year. For some, this relationship will last a lifetime. For good or ill, I will be the first teacher in their school career and set the tone that will shape their lives and mine for years to come.

After almost twenty "first days of school," I've learned what to expect. Any minute now, I am anticipating at least one of Snow White's seven little friends—*Happy, Doc, Sleepy, Dopey, Bashful, Sneezy*, and *Grumpy*—to walk through my door. Some will be like innocent little *Happy*, bubbling with joy for no apparent reason. The little *Docs* will be almost ready for second grade (at least according to their mothers). For various reasons, others will show up, like *Sleepy,* with less than the required hours of sleep and take full advantage of "quiet time." Then there is the lovable little *Dopey.* He just doesn't have a clue, and it won't be the last time in his life that he'll hear "bless his heart." Of course, cute little *Bashful* will slink in without ever looking up, and you can bet that her friend Sneezy will need the services of the school nurse before the day ends. This merry band of children wouldn't be complete without little *Grumpy,* who will find something to whine about in the first five minutes of his school career. For the next 180 days, these will be "my" children with whom I get to go off to work each day, if not whistling, at least smiling.

I am continually reminded of how important each one is. The words in red ink in an old book I read remind me of how serious my charge is, "...whosoever shall offend one of these little ones...it is better that a millstone were hanged about his neck and he were drowned in the depth of the sea" (Matthew 18:6). They are indeed God's babies—the good ones, the mean ones, the loud ones, and the quiet ones—all of them. I am, in fact, His babies' keeper. So, I best be ready.

For so many reasons, it matters how I treat each of them. To paraphrase an old Sunday school song I learned long ago, "they are precious in *my* sight," and like Jesus, yes, I love them. Now, if you'll excuse me, I have to finish my preparation. It's a big day. As *Doc* would tell you, there's no second chance for a kid's first day of school.

september 8

Cutting Up Has Consequences

A woman who cuts her hair is about to change her life.

Coco Chanel

It's now early September, and we've almost settled into a rhythm. For the most part, they know *where* to put things in the closet, but they're still working on getting it done. Like my friends and me in the grown-up world, they generally have good intentions. These little darlings are also a lot like us in other ways. Most of us have learned, sometimes painfully, that an idea that seems to make sense in the darker corners of our brains can fall apart in the daylight of reality. These harsh lessons are taught every day in school, especially in kindergarten.

The big lessons in life are usually learned best by people unafraid of trying new and sometimes dangerous things, at least dangerous to our tender egos. Kids are fearless and don't seem to mind being wrong. Unfortunately, most of us relapse with age. While time may wound all heels, gratefully, it also heals all wounds. Often things work out when you take chances.

One of the big chances we take early in kindergarten

is putting scissors in the tiny hands of kids who can't tie their shoes. For some crazy reason, with cognitive processing patterns, cutting with scissors connects to early reading ability. Consequently, we break out the scissors early and often. Like early reading, the educational benchmark, "cuts with scissors," is unevenly distributed, at least in my class.

So, this morning, I distributed the scissors box, some yellow and brown construction paper, and several tubs of white paste. As patiently as I could, I covered the fundamentals, which finger fits in what hole and how scissors open and close. Experienced kindergarten teachers and most moms know that my following line is critical, *scissors are for paper, not for clothes, and not for hair!!*

Somehow, most of the children have managed to cut out the semblance of a square, triangle, and circle they traced on the yellow construction paper. Without a lot of grief, most managed to get a blob of glue on at least some of the paper and stick it to the big brown sheet.

Using what I learned a while back from Marvin Gaye and maybe an Educational Psychology class or two, I smoothly transitioned into a math lesson by having them count the number of shapes. Lev Vygotsky, Jacob Kounin, and of course, my man Marvin would have been so proud. As I'm patrolling the tiny tables watching kids with tools they shouldn't run with or carry on an airplane, I'm congratulating myself on this seamless transition (what Kounin would call *overlapping*). With scissors in one hand and tiny fingers poking at squares and circles that were neither squares nor circles, they were counting under their breath with the seriousness of a judge.

After school, I cleaned up a lot of unintended and a few intended messes. Then I find a thatch of curly hair by Eloise's desk on the floor, and I immediately know to whom this hair sample belongs. I had to call her parents, but I was not thrilled. Phone calls after school are about as much fun to make as they are to get.

Dad answered, and I stumbled through my version of the events. I was pleasantly surprised when he said with what sounded like a smile, "It's okay. She tried that at home as well." As Eloise noted later, "It seemed right." But I had to remind this young cosmetology student that this is kindergarten, not *Great Clips*. By Halloween, you couldn't tell what had happened from the *outside*. My hunch is that a permanent life lesson was learned somewhere *inside*, and maybe an early reading lesson. We teachers do work that matters, although we can't always see it.

september 15

Gender Equity May Have Limits

Ready. Fire. Aim.

*Anyone of a host of ineffective
administrators*

Today, I learned that gender equality has unintended consequences. I also discovered that my survival kit for kindergarten was missing a valuable addition that has made a big difference in the personal hygiene of my students and me. To truly understand it, you will have to appreciate the significant gender inequality in my class this year. Most of us know that females are generally about 51% of the population. Not in my room. Not this year. I have five beautiful little girls and fourteen (as in almost three times more) rambunctious little boys.

If you missed the significance of that arithmetic, you would know it by the smell of urine in our class's bathroom. After three weeks of school, none of us has gone "nose blind." More than once, I've seen little boys' sneakers untied and automatically bent down to retie soaking wet laces. Before "the rabbit goes around and comes back through the hole," I've figured out why they're wet.

Y'all, it's a stinking, sinking feeling. I've tried everything. *Renuzit* didn't, *Mr. Clean* went on strike, and *Baby Wipes* were not big enough. I needed help. I asked our male custodian to have a "man talk" with the little boys about staying *inside* the bowl. Some were not even in the same zip code. After "the talk," it got a little better, they were at least in the right neighborhood, but it was still a problem.

To prepare for our first PTA meeting, I chose the nuclear option—a gallon of bleach with a Pine-Sol chaser. Trying desperately to explain the overwhelming odor, I danced around the issue. A wise father raised his hand and enlightened most of us in the room. With what sounded like a wink in his voice, he summed up my problem.

Reassuringly he said, "I know you are aiming to please, but these boys need to aim too, please." He continued, "At our house, we put a fruit loop in the toilet, and it became target practice. Problem solved."

I thought I was listening to one of the Oracles at Delphi. I had an epiphany or something close to it. Who knew cereal could help my class pass our weekly *smelling* test? As a result of my learning, I added stale *Fruit Loops* to my kindergarten survival kit.

September 24

A New Year and Fresh Starts

New beginnings happen every day.

My Pastor

G ood morning, and Happy "New Year" from my *new* bunch and me! It may be September, but it "feels" like a new year, except it's warm, and nobody's singing that aggravating song about an ancient man with an odd name, *Aude Lang Syne* (apparently, his mama didn't want children). Anyway, we've been out of school a while. Hurricane Florence blew into town a couple of weeks ago, and schools were closed in her honor. The more resourceful ones of us organized a boat parade.

Naturally, the last two weeks were a disaster, literally. But the world turns, and today is a new beginning—for my little ones and me. All but one of my tiny chickadees found the nest this morning, and I can thankfully report that the missing child is okay. After what we've seen the last few days, none of us are counting "the sniffles."

"Flo" changed all of us. It seemed like one of those "teachable moments," so I decided to explore, "How are we different after the hurricane?" We were going to make a collage of our deeply personal experiences using cut-out pictures from my collection of old magazines and glue them on poster board. A teacher's great idea does not always go as planned like in real life.

To pull off my educational goal, my first order of business was to glove up (glue bottles and life are messy) and perform a common technical procedure, most often due to neglect. When we left days ago, our big glue bottle was left uncapped and exposed to the elements. Like most of us, the glue hardens when it is ignored, and in those circumstances and in that condition, it's useless. As my kindergartners know, the soft stuff left in the bottom of the bottle was no good if we couldn't get past the hard layer on top. So, I had to find a sharp pointy instrument and *jab* (I think that too is a medical term) it into the hole of our glue bottle. As the kids correctly pointed out, it was only after the blockage was cleared that could we get on with our activity that revealed stories of other life-changing lessons learned in a disaster.

Here are some things I learned. Every day is a new beginning, a brand new, fresh-out-of-the-box day. Sadly, most of us never notice. A line from Kung Fu Panda said it best, "Yesterday is history. Tomorrow's a mystery. Today is a gift; that's why they call it the present." We are too easily distracted by external events beyond our control and ignore our responsibilities to celebrate each new day. That attitude helps keep the gooey goodness in all of us flowing out to where it can do what it is supposed to. We can't dry up and get crusty and stopped up. When that happens, it may take an uncomfortable procedure to scrape off our hard exteriors to get to the good stuff that holds us together.

The Shapes in Learning Matter

The child is father to the man.

William Wordsworth,
My Heart Leaps Up

In a time when there is so much going on in the world, as the mayor of Kinderville, I wanted to try at least to solve one problem to help the world. As we all know, shapes matter to us in everything from choosing a mate to reading. In Kinderville, we're not that concerned about the former, but we're all about the latter. If you have a driver's license, you probably know way too much about the relationship between shapes and marriage choices already, so I'll leave that to you. However, we spend a lot of time in Kinderville deciphering letter shapes and their meanings in a designed effort to build a solid foundation for reading. The number of humps on an "M" can mean the difference between what a cat says, "Meow," and a description of Mama's *new* boyfriend. This kind of acute discrimination in the shape of letters helps us make sense of words and, ultimately, the world.

It's about two months into this new kindergarten year, and it's apparent that the residents of Kinderville are having a little problem distinguishing the shape of the lowercase "b" and "d." If we are honest, most of us have struggled with that same thing at some point. Still, I can tell you it's a familiar and persistent problem here in Kinderville. I suspect out there in the suburbs as well.

Good news! I've done a little research, and I'm happy to report my findings. According to the imminent scholar "Dr. Pintrest" (she seems to know everything!), here's the skinny. It was a poster, so I'll try to describe it. The "b" was a baby with a diaper hanging just below a cute little belly button. The "d" was a baby with a diaper covering a tiny round bottom with a stinky cartoon bubble coming out of the "hinder parts." I showed it to the Kinderville residents, and we all had a big laugh.

Another problem was solved. Now, most of us can tell the difference between "dad" and "bad," and we all know that the diaper covers make a real difference. I think I heard several light switches being flipped on, including one in the far corner of my head. Where was "Dr. Pinterest" when I was in kindergarten? Maybe I could have read my bubble double gum wrapper.

October 6

A Teacher's Superpower

I suppose that to a large extent, I am the unsigned manuscript of that teacher. What deathless power lies in the hands of such a person.

John Steinbeck describing his favorite teacher

Most of us have wished for at least one superpower at some point in our lives. As a teacher, I've had days when Superman's x-ray vision, Iron Man's freeze ray, or Dr. Strange's ability to clone himself would undoubtedly have come in handy. These abilities are certainly appealing to a tired and worn-out accountant, and I know they'd be a real asset in a kindergarten classroom.

I'd have to be dreaming to think something like that could ever happen to me. But now that I think about it, if you don't count Tom Brady and a few nights out in a crowded theater, I've never seen a superhero in real life up close and personal. That is until today.

This morning Michael showed up with a present. With his goofy toothless grin, he proudly announced that it was from his momma and "It's for you, Ms. Hardaway!" I proudly took the plain cardboard box wrapped with twine. Inside was a beautiful bright fuchsia T-shirt, my favorite color! Yeah! More importantly, there was an *Avengers* homemade drawing with superheroes talking about teachers and how they too had superpowers. The words written in the word bubbles were not graded for correct spelling. Consonants and vowels were everywhere, yet I understood it all.

I was totally surprised! Okay, I'll admit I may have mentioned the *Avengers* movie a couple of times (a day); however, as it turns out, it was a passion Michael and I shared. He was an avid fan! Mike explained that, like Thor, "Teachers too have superpowers and can change a kid's way of thinking." He drew the Black Panther, Captain America, and some of their other super friends and excitingly explained that teachers help kids use their own super powers to figure out what is going on in the world. The more I read these lines, the stronger I felt, and the bigger Michael's eyes got. We were both really into it. I don't mean to get all Pentecostal on you, but y'all, I actually began to feel super-power-*ish*. For a few seconds, my eyes narrowed, and I *was* an *Avenger* (one of the good ones, though).

My transformation quickly unraveled when little Leah timidly tugged on my dress. I turned and proudly bent down—ready to leap small buildings in a single bound. It was then I realized there was one super-power missing on my new *Avengers* picture, teeth pulling.

October 11

Hard Sounds in Soft Answers

Life is what happens while we're busy making other plans.

Allen Saunders

After a leisurely Sunday afternoon of trying to digest some good strong preaching, it was time to turn my thoughts toward what the next week would be like in my kindergarten class. We are beginning readers, so we learn about hard and soft sounds. Consequently, my old tried and true text, *Phonics with a Very Hungry Caterpillar,* sounded like a winner.

I went to bed Sunday night thinking about the odd notion that letters can sound differently based on other letters around them. For instance, "C" can sound like the letter "K" as in "can," "cat," and "cap." Or it can sound like the letter "S" as in "ice," "cellar," and "census." It all depends on circumstances in that particular letter's neighborhood. The English language is full of exceptions. Anyway, I slept well and woke up ready to take on changing letter sounds. Little did I know that I was the one who would get an education on complex sounds that Monday morning.

When I signed in this morning, the secretary handed me a note with a hospital phone number. The look on her face indicated the "urgency" (with a soft "C"). I talked with a mom who was still trying to process the rapid progression of her baby's disease. It was a hard "C" word that neither of us could get past the lump in our throats. Of course, I hadn't given birth to that child, but that morning he belonged to both of us. Since August, I've helped feed him, watched him learn how paste works, introduced him to the hard "C" letter sound that's now threatening his life, and mostly prayed for him every day. I felt at least some of that mom's raw anguish. Like most of my colleagues, each of my students finds a soft spot in my heart where they set up shop and gnaws at my innards. What happens to them after the last bell sounds matters to me.

After the kids settled in and the morning announcements were made, I gave them a worksheet on some soft and hard "C" sounds and quietly slipped off to the cloakroom where I secretly dialed up "The Royal Telephone" and talked to Jesus. I did not birth that little boy personally, but I sure prayed like I did. I don't know if my little student felt better that morning, but I certainly did. I came out of that closet humming an old gospel tune, "Just a Little Talk with Jesus Makes it Right."

As I reflected on that morning, I realized I was the student. I learned that adults also have a lot of trouble with the complications of hard "C" words. I also learned that the soft "C" word "grace" could be one of the most effective tools in managing the real-life issues that trouble my students and me outside of the class. No matter what happens, we are all children of a God of love who extends the gift of two soft "C" words, "grace" and "peace," to anyone who will take it regardless of circumstance. May it be so.

October 14

Nobody Misses School Like Parents

---

*You don't know what you've got till
it's gone...*

Mama

After a short visit along the South Carolina coast, an angry Hurricane Matthew came roaring into town on Saturday, dripping wet. Apparently, he got angry at our inhospitable attitude—some had boarded up their windows and doors when they heard he was coming. Undeterred, he came anyway and, by the way, blew in a lot of doors. The first day he dumped about fifteen inches of rain in our community and, I think, hung around a few more days out of spite. The resulting flood shut down areas in and around Fayetteville for the next six days. Schools reopened as soon as the floodwaters receded enough to get the fish off the courthouse lawn. My twenty-two babies had been trapped inside their houses with their *other* parents 24/7 for the last six days. As many moms and dads told me, a five and six-year-old child's questions are cute for the first couple of days, but like some houseguests, they wear thin after a while. To keep the peace and perhaps more than a few parents out of jail, schools had to reopen yesterday.

Oh, the joys of coming back to school after being out a week and then throwing in a storm! This morning was festive. My colleagues and I were in the hall next to my door, ready to welcome our babies back. Genuinely warm and broad smiles were plastered on everyone's faces. We were happy to see our kids, and they seemed more than pleased to be back. But the biggest grins were those on the faces of the people walking their children down the hall. It could have been our home-made "Welcome Back" signs, or perhaps the Dr. Seuss hats that some wore, or maybe it was that today was Friday. All I know is that moms and dads were way too excited about dropping off these little "question boxes." Even Tyler's mom, who never smiled, was almost giddy. She even asked about me. For the first time, some of the parents looked at my colleagues and me as stage partners in this vital act in their child's life. For a brief and shining moment, I felt as if I worked at Camelot Elementary School. I even think I heard one of the parents pledge his fealty in Lancelot's tender version of "If Ever I Would Leave You."

October 17

My Scents and Time are Not Universal

Time moves slowly but passes quickly.

Alice Walker

We seem to be an impatient bunch. We simply can't wait. It used to take a couple of hours to cook a square meal. Then TV taught us that a crime could be committed, investigated, and solved in less than an hour, and of course, we had to have a meal that could be ready before the credits rolled. Enter the aptly named TV dinner. It was literally a square meal that could be ready before the second commercial. The problem was that that took at least a half-hour. It was evident that nobody has that kind of time in the modern world. After all, this ain't Bedrock, and we're not the Flintstones.

An enterprising cookware salesman saw an opening and introduced "fast food." You could drive by the place and, in about eight minutes, be in and out with a burger and fries. Honestly, who has eight minutes? To save time and speed up our indigestion, some thoughtful person knocked a hole in the side of the building. We could then drive through and pick up burgers and fries or at least another customer's onion rings in an average of two minutes.

It seems that we've come to expect that same kind of immediacy in human development. Our kids are growing up fast, probably too fast. I suppose that's been said in every generation, but it seems especially true nowadays. If I ask my students how old they are, most will focus on the following year, as in, "I'll be six my next *burfday*." Kindergarten used to be about learning life skills like staying in the lines and afternoon naps. Now naps are so 20th century, so analog in a digital world. In my 21st century classroom, my babies take entrance placement exams for kindergarten. Unfortunately, in my opinion, there's simply not enough time devoted to just "playing."

Most of us don't have the ability to delay gratification, one of the four central elements of what Duckworth called "grit." In a society built on immediacy, we want things right now! We just can't wait. "How can I get my child through the four cognitive stages faster?" was a question that the preeminent child psychologist Jean Piaget called "the American Question." He hated it. His advice to antsy parents was, "Let kids be kids..." after all, "play is serious business." To Piaget's dismay, adults hurry children through stages that have so many important lessons to teach. Parents send me little people with their mom's and dad's big ideas and expectations neatly rolled up in their little lunch boxes. Sometimes it's more overt than that.

This is the first year I've dealt with parents sending their sons to my class smelling like a grown man who spent too much time at Macy's cologne counter. Don't get me wrong; I like cologne. I've spent a little time at the Macy's counter myself. I can even recognize some of the overpriced fancy mysterious scents with funny-sounding names and ads that oversell the product.

This morning I was shocked, and I don't shock easily. I thought I smelled a grown man walking through the door. I looked around, and the only thing in the door was Julian, a snaggle-toothed child. He was cute, but he still colored with fat crayons. It was too much!

That morning, Julian's "scent" could've been a cheap knockoff fragrance with a package that reads "If you like Ralph Lauren Polo..." on the label. It could've been the real thing! It could've been the real thing! That got me thinking. My kids don't need to smell like the rapper Common (the way he smiles says, "I smell good"). He's grown. If kids must wear cologne, I have a hint for the smart people who make stuff. Instead of "It smells just like Obsession," it might be better if it smelled like something they could pronounce. In that vein, some catchy package copy would say something like, *If You Like Legos*, or maybe *Tonka Trucks*, perhaps *Elmer's Glue*, or maybe *GI Joe*. I'm still trying to teach Ray how to color in the lines. I don't need my nose asking, "Can we go to Applebee's?"

October 18

Lessons in Sidewalk Sight Words

You need to let the little things that would ordinarily bore you suddenly thrill you.

Andy Warhol

On the sidewalk, waiting for the afternoon late bus, a few of my babies had a Sidewalk Chalk Party and invited the teacher! I was frankly a little surprised but honored. We all knelt on the hot concrete, drew funny pictures, and tested each other with sight words I had assigned that morning. One challenge led to another, and before I knew it, I got snookered in Tic-Tac-Toe too many times for a teacher. But I was into it. In less time than it takes a little one to tell you what happened in the cafeteria last Tuesday, I was a mess. I had chalk on my hands, and as Jeanie timidly pointed out, a few stray lime green marks on my face. Like I say, I was into it. We laughed.

It—all of it—was surprisingly relaxing and enjoyable. Before I knew it, I had lost track of time and found my long day's anxiety melting away. Just then, the other adult on bus duty announced bus forty-three. I probably stood up too quickly. I saw some beautiful pictures but not on the sidewalk. Thankfully, these colorful stars that only I could see went away sooner than the sidewalk sight words. That bright October afternoon, I learned a couple of critical terminal objectives that were not written out in my lesson plan for the day. First, after forty, it may be best to take at least as much time getting up as it takes to get down. Secondly, I learned my sight word for the day, *serendipity*. Unplanned happy accidents are powerful teachers for kids of all ages.

October 21

Love Weighs a Lot

Love is when you feel good because you have someone who is always with you.

Madelynne, 6 years old

In the life of a kindergarten teacher, there's at least one "Oh my goodness!" moment or, as my grandmother would say, "Lord have mercy!!!" Today it was Malik's turn. He probably started kindergarten too early and will likely be given another year to get it right. He's a quiet, sweet little boy who rarely speaks unless I ask him about something. I suspect it's his stuttering that keeps him on the sidelines.

At recess a couple of days ago, I noticed that the group he usually hung around with was pointing and laughing; that is all except Malik. I sashayed over in that direction, and while I was watching the girls play, I listened to the boys. One had asked about Malik's daddy, and he wanted to tell them, but he couldn't seem to get past the "L" in "locked up." The harder he tried, the worse he stammered and the funnier it was to the growing crowd of children around him.

I ached for him. With one finger, I summoned him to

an important "teacher meeting." Kneeling, I dabbed at tears swelling up in the corner of his big dark eyes. Quietly I said, "Malik, I'd like to know about your family if you want to tell me." Of course, I knew, but I wanted to give him some space, let it be his decision. Without looking up, he mouthed, okay, and we made a plan.

Honestly, I was unsure what that plan would look like or even what I *should* do. What I did know was that after two decades of paying attention to little children, "be there" and "shut up" is often the best medicine for wounded children. To "be there" is pretty easy—I'm contractually obligated; however, as a real talkative type, I'm still working on the "shut up" part.

So, after recess, I called his mom and asked her to pick him up about thirty minutes later. After school, kids collected lunch boxes, straightened their desks for tomorrow's class, and hurried toward the door. Malik hung back. When the last child finally shuffled out, Malik was in the chair beside my desk, swinging his feet and fidgeting with papers on the corner of my desk.

The conversation began easy enough. The Panthers had won on Sunday. I let him tell me all about Cam Newton as I worked on keeping quiet. Of course, he occasionally struggled with certain letters and phrases, but I noticed that as he got more comfortable, words tumbled out of him like an Appalachian waterfall.

We talked some about his family and the hardship of daddy's absence, and all I did was smile and occasionally mumble something like, "Oh my goodness," "No!" "Really?" All the while, Malik was emptying his belly of a lot of rotting sentences and finding some level of acceptance. He finally stopped talking when his mom came to the door. The sad little kid I sat down with was smiling again and looking directly at me. I'm sure that his half-hour in the spotlight did not completely heal the deep gashes left by years of hateful words, but it did look as if they may be beginning to scar over.

As we walked to the door, he latched onto me as if one of us was leaving for Australia forever. He looked up at me and gave me what makes almost anything better— a dead serious hug. It was an eloquent "thank you!" for my "being there." Without a smile and searching for the most significant modifier he knew, Malik said, "Ms. Hardaway, I love you, a hundred pounds!" At that point, a little water leaked out of one of my eyes. It occurred to me that I had been toe to toe with a real heavyweight in love.

October 26

Honesty May Be a Good Policy, But It's a Lousy Pick-Up Line

Intoxicated people, children, and leggings always tell the truth.

Zina Harrington

Most kids love their kindergarten teacher and are generally compelled to say so. Unfortunately for my thin-skinned colleagues, the little ones are truth-telling machines. They "call 'em like they see 'em." Sometimes even their honest compliments can sting a little. On the kid's side of these frequent conversations, their version of the simple, unfiltered truth, though limited by their worldview, is meant as a sincere expression of devotion.

These conversations are like a ping-pong match between a young "natural" athlete and one that long ago may have been a star. Out of the blue, the child, a natural at this kind of give and take, will say something, and then I try to return the serve. Unfortunately, my skills are hamstrung by filters of politeness and political correctness. My "opponent" in this match is not so constrained. He tells his truth without any toppings, with no spin, or the mental editing often necessary in adult conversations. These honest-to-goodness talks are delightful, and like C.S. Lewis, I'm often "surprised by joy." Sometimes I'm just so flabbergasted that I can't return a ball that's squarely in my court. Perhaps a long time ago, I would have been a better partner in this game. As I've gotten older, I've learned way too much about what you're supposed to say. Here are a couple of recent examples.

Scene 1: We are learning to cut and paste the old-fashioned way—no electronic devices required. On a squatty table are a variety of old magazines, tubs of white paste, and a coffee can full of tiny dull scissors. Sitting around the table are a bunch of eager artists ready to make a fall collage. We're into it.

She: "Ms. Hardaway, how old are you?"

Me: Shocked, I put down a wooden tongue depressor thick with paste and, with my best-practiced smile, said, "How old do I look?"

She: (The little girl comes over, squats down beside my seat, and proceeds to use her hand as a scanner and "scans" me from the top of my head to the bottom of my shoes. All the while, she's counting and suddenly stops at nineteen). "You are nineteen!" she proudly announced.

Me: "Sweetie, add a few more years! I'm thirty-nine years old."

She: (Pauses, looks at me with a big smile, and adds), "You know what? … and you're so straight and tall!"

Me: "Thank you, baby! Yes, I'm so proud to be nineteen and so "straight and tall!'"

Scene 2: I'm sitting at my desk grading writing papers. A few of my students are standing around silently, watching me work. Suddenly, I feel a little hand rubbing my arm. I stopped to see who it was. No surprise this time. It's our class's gap-toothed "Romeo," a self-avowed, five-year-old "ladies' man."

He: (With practiced sweetness, he says) "Ms. Hardaway, you're so *cushy.*"

Me: I had nothing. The only response I could manage was silence. I pursed my lips and gave him my best used car salesman smile. Without saying it, I thought, cushy? Ouch! You don't say cushy to a woman, not now and certainly not later. As I understand the term, it must be kindergarten for thick boned! I guess he'll learn the hard way that cushy is probably not the most effective pick-up line. Score a point for the little Romeo "wannabe."

November 4

The Teaching/Learning Equation

Involves New Math

---

*If it seems easy, you must be doing it
wrong.*

Uncle Carroll

I t's Friday, and I'm grateful, fried, but grateful.
Today we tried to solve one of those math problems that begins on one blackboard and ends on
another—*Good Will Hunting* style. Tomorrow
morning and probably for the rest of the weekend,
I'll smell like a tub of Icy Hot with a touch of vine-
gar, but I digress. Let's do the math first.

One of my professors pointed out that math is not my
strong suit. At my level, we do a lot of "carrying" (a few
numbers, but mostly kids) and a little of the arithmetic
that has something to do with an apple pie cut into
slices. My math teachers always claimed that math's
just not that complex, but the long formulas scared me
for some reason. Numbers aren't the only thing that
can be irrational.

The best I can figure, math is like trying out a new
cornbread recipe, but all the measurements are in

50

metric units. I don't claim to be the best cook, but I know enough about eating to appreciate that the quantity of each ingredient matters. For those who may not know our way around a kitchen, what comes out of the oven in these conditions is generally a surprise. Most of my Fridays are like that. We use that day to try new things, celebrate big events, and learn things just for the fun of it. Today was Friday.

Here's the irrational recipe I wrestled with today. Six hertz of a birthday party, add two dozen bytes of cupcakes, fold in one square centimeter of *Despicable Me*, a half-liter of bubble stuff with twenty-two plastic devices to blow through, and a gross (I don't think that's a metric measurement, but it fits) of glue sticks. At this point, add the reminder, "We don't eat glue sticks.").

What came out of all of that was indeed a bunch of pleasant surprises—hilarious conversations with my children, not the least of which was a five-year-old's perspective on why he's voting for Bernie Sanders (it was something about his hair). Don't even ask me how we came to that discussion. The other kind of painful benefit was that on the way out of the door that afternoon, I got a bunch of serious hugs, the kind that would squeeze the pulp out of a green orange, but it was nothing a little *Icy Hot* and taking my shoes off won't fix. Tonight, I'll rest soundly. Factoring in the surprises, it seems to me that today all of us have made some progress in the world's most important problem to solve, the teaching and learning equation.

There's an Answer For Everything (Sometimes It's Right)

For every problem under the sun,

There is an answer, or there is none.

If there is one, seek till you find it.

If there is none, never mind it.

Mother Goose

One can learn a lot on a farm. Some of our most enduring lessons have come directly from these places where men and women are engaged in a delicate dance with Mother Nature. In life's most basic terms, farmers tease out a living for themselves and us from the great cycles of life that feed and clothe us. There are life lessons to be taught and learned at each stage on the farm.

A farm is a place where life and death are confronted daily with powerful implications for our own struggles. It's a nursery of dreams and potential and sometimes heartbreak. These fundamental lessons on living and dying are taught by a variety of species who can't talk, and while they may know their name, they certainly can't spell it.

Our favorite teachers on the farm come in all shapes and sizes, and they have played a significant role in our general education. Those who've never actually seen a cow pie have learned a lot from Mother Goose, The Little Red Hen, cows jumping over the moon, and the three little pigs who took a crack at the house construction business. As one in the teaching and learning enterprise, it made sense that we take our kindergarten classes on a field trip to the font of our general knowledge, a working farm.

With free-range chickens and a couple of smelly but friendly goats in supporting roles, our teacher and host this day was one of the animals on the farm who could talk, an old cotton farmer. He gave us the warmest welcome this side of Mayberry. He had our children right from the start when he explained that contrary to what Old McDonald said, "farm" was not spelled EIEIO.

When the laughter died down, he gave each child a cotton boll as an "advanced organizer" for his talk on the south's staple crop. He talked us through the details of the life cycle of the seeds in the soft white fibrous bundle. He may have mentioned Eli Whitney a time or two, but I wasn't listening too closely. I was corralling a few stray five-year-olds who had wandered off from the herd.

As he was closing, he asked for other alternative uses for this white fluffy substance, and he got lots of suggestions from his eager audience. Tiny hands shot up like popcorn across the old barn. I think it must be the smell of the barnyard that gets the creative juices flowing, but I guess if a milk cow can jump over a moon, anything is possible. Perhaps the most energetic was Jamal. He suggested that the stuff he was holding was maybe the main ingredient in one of his favorites, Cotton Candy. Quickly, another child added that he had it on good authority that this was the main thing in his grandma's toilet paper. Lots of other ideas followed, and none of them came from Siri. For a brief moment in time, the possibilities seemed endless.

December 1

Teachers are Always on Duty

Be Prepared.

Boy Scout Motto

A plumber is always a plumber. They think about *flow* and its patterns more than Csikszentmihalyi, the guy who wrote the book on it. The plumber's highly trained skills are portable and can be unpacked with similar results in my house or Dunkin Donuts. The surroundings do not impact the expensive skill set they bring to the job site. They work in almost any location at any time. Before you pay the plumber's bill (that would finance a smartboard), the clog is cleared, and things are running again.

A chef is always a chef. If you are standing behind one in the checkout line at Advanced Auto, they can tell you exactly how to cook fettuccine alfredo without burning the sauce, and you won't have to buy that fancy hat.

A teacher is always a teacher. At family reunions or around dinner tables, they are more likely to notice incorrect grammar usage. Some teachers who take themselves too seriously may offer unwanted corrections or "constructive criticism" that could solve the problem. Like plumbers and chefs, teachers are always on duty.

The skillset seems to accompany the skilled one everywhere. Our job is to take full advantage of those rare "teachable moments."

This past Saturday, I was in J.C. Penny's, and although I didn't have a dry erase marker on me, a lesson was about to be taught. A learning set was taking shape.

Teaching is not so much what we do. It's who we are all the time. We work nights, weekends, and holidays. We're always on duty, especially in the thin slice of our content specialty. English teachers hear things (e.g., subject/verb agreement) that others don't, Science teachers can get a little irritated that the rest of us can't get the Krebs Cycle, and kindergarten teachers seem to know when a child is about to explode.

Teachers make a living anticipating problems. As a way of maintaining discipline in their classrooms, the good ones practice Barney Fife's "nip it in the bud" philosophy. Classroom teachers know this practice as Jacob Kounin's classic term, "with-it-ness." We all know that students are not likely to learn numbers, fractions, or differential equations if the class is in chaos. Consequently, we have developed a nose for trouble, and we are not afraid to use it. Teachers can almost sense when things are about to unravel at school or almost anywhere else. It's as if teachers have some sort of superpower.

Penny's was packed with holiday shoppers. It was holiday picture time, and mom and dad were wrangling kids in the direction of the Olan Mills Studio. My eye caught a little freckled-faced boy plotting his escape from his mom and dad. Unfortunately, the little boy had spotted toys in an aisle not that far away. While most of my fellow shoppers clearly heard momma's anxious calls, the siren call of the toys was louder.

He had previously done his homework, and he knew the shortest route between the picture line and the toy aisle. What he didn't see was my automatic antennae rising well before he bolted, and he certainly didn't hear the universal bat signal to all nearby teachers. After a couple of decades of anticipating the sudden movements of little children, I knew that I had to answer this bat call.

While mom was fumbling for the right card to cover the family package that included eight wallet sizes and a 11X14 framed matt finish, dad was scrolling through his phone, hoping he was needed back at the plant.

The tiny fugitive saw his opening. He broke past dad in a dead run toward the big yellow Tonka truck parked a couple of aisles over. Immediately, my arm morphed into a railroad crossing signal and stopped him in his tracks. I didn't even have time to find a phone booth and change clothes, and gratefully, I didn't have to put on that smelly blue cape (It's not been cleaned since the Bush administration. The first one). This was relatively light duty for a teacher, and perhaps for a dish of fettuccine alfredo, I'll teach you how.

December 6

The Job's Not Done Until the Paperwork is Done

It has long been an axiom of mine that little things are infinitely most important.

Sir Author Conan Doyle

Good morning! We are slowly inching our way toward the halfway point in this academic year. By now, I thought my children had a pretty good handle on the basic classroom rules. I was wrong. As the bouncy tunes at the mall incessantly remind us, Christmas break is just around the corner, so close you can almost smell it. Unfortunately, I'm not talking about the pine boughs in my window or the faint smell of glue left over from our Christmas tree ornament projects. It's time for an emergency life lesson for these cute little children on the other side of my desk.

This is a chance for you to play along at home and guess what my lesson this morning includes. Nope, not about how to make snowflakes or how to make things grow. Not even about how to make an at-home aquarium. Sorry, but thanks for playing. Please pick up your lovely parting gifts on the way out.

Staying with the "lovely parting gifts" theme, my lesson was about how to ensure that Ms. Hardaway never has to clean up behind her short, snaggletooth kinder people in the potty anymore! The lesson included an anticipatory set, context-specific objectives, many low-road transfer issues, and various integrated disciplines. Basic physics and trajectory were spiraled down to how aiming at the target is an important part of hitting it. The science of economics was also included with budgetary questions on the costs of Clorox Wipes and the number required to clean up little puddles that should be in the toilet. We even included elements of our responsibility to the Earth with a discussion of how many trees give their lives for wasted toilet paper on the floor.

As some of my older friends reminded me, accidents happen, but sometimes we are just careless. Humans, by nature, are messy people, but our toilet is not a gas station bathroom. The trick is to minimize the damage of accidents by taking personal responsibility. It's easier, cheaper, and more responsible for each of us to wipe up tiny accidents than to ignore them. Thankfully, my children seem to understand better how to answer me when I ask, "Is my bathroom clean?" All-day long, the answer was, "Yes, Mam!"

Of course, you probably won't find this lesson plan on

Pinterest. Consequently, I'm available to lead potty etiquette workshops for people with tiny feet. Like my students, I aim to please, but I expect my students to aim too, please. My number is 1-800-CLEAN UP.

December 8

Loud, Innocent Smiles are Contagious

---

*While parents possess the original key
to their offspring's experience,
teachers have a spare key.*

Hiam Ginott

O nce a baby enters the world, everything the child needs to be the best is already there. Developing and training can undoubtedly shape and sharpen it, but the raw material is present. That's easy to understand in the mornings when everything is just right. Those mornings I rise and shine, usually humming a jaunty Mary Poppins tune before my first cup of coffee.

Other mornings are different. Sometimes the old man on the Quaker Oates box seems to look at me as if to say, "Fix your face and your attitude, and there *better* be a difference by the time I'm done cooking!"

No matter how I feel in the mornings, these little faces at work will expect me to walk in with a parrot head umbrella that can transport all of us to Ms. Frizzle's "Magic School Bus" that first existed in the mind of Peter Lurye. Mostly when I least expect it, there are days when the magic does happen, and I do get to ride that

63

bus with a child and watch the universe take its course, and there's absolutely nothing I can do about it. This was one of those days.

I first saw her this morning walking down the hall in our wing. Even at a distance, it was clear that this thin little girl was *special* in every sense of the word. She was in another kindergarten class, but I had learned a lot about her in the teacher's lounge. To tell the truth, even though we had never officially met, I had a tinge of jealousy that I was not her "real teacher."

This sweet little bright-eyed girl loved and laughed easily. According to the teacher talk, she'd spontaneously break out in a joyful dance to music that only she heard. She never cared who was looking or where the class was in the lesson plan. Real joy is hard to hide. That morning, her hair was fixed in short pigtails and tied with once bright pink ribbons. As she danced down the hall, our eyes met. Her face cracked open with a smile that would burn a hole right through the hardest heart. I think I *heard* it echo off our brightly colored block walls.

I knelt and opened my arms to intercept her. Breathlessly and with intense pride, she straightened up, folded her arms, and declared, "My name is Latisha, but Mama calls me Tish."

I said, "Good morning, Ms. Sunshine!"

Unbelievably, her smile widened, and with big bright

dark eyes staring right into mine, she innocently ex-claimed, "Hey, you're brown like me!"

Proudly, I said, "Baby, you're absolutely right! I sure am!"

After comparing skin tones, she cracked open her prize-winning smile again, said "bye-bye," and danced on down the hall.

After that, it was a ritual. Tish would find me almost every morning, and when the music in her head would pause, she'd hug me tight. Although I was not her teacher, she indeed did become mine. She taught me that some things matter and some don't. She taught me that limits imposed by a serious diagnosis or our exaggerated titles are artificial, that real, honest-to-goodness joy is impossible to keep inside. It must be shared. Most of all, Ms. Tish taught me that an inno-cent smile is contagious, especially the *loud* ones.

December 9

Just Because Johnny Can't Read Doesn't Mean He Can't Sing

"Santa Claus is Coming to Town"

Fred Coots and Haven Gillespie

The Christmas season is in full swing. We've already started the countdown until the big day when some say that a fat guy in red flannel breaks into everybody's house, not to take things (if you don't count a few stale chocolate chip cookies from the bread store), but—get this—he leaves stuff.

Somehow, soft instrumental tunes morph into sappy traditional songs that worm themselves into the brain. We all become singers, even Elmo and Patsy. Actually, they shouldn't count because they're professionals. As most in these parts will tell you, the days till this blessed event are negatively related to the times radio plays Elmo and Patsy's big hit "Grandma Got Run Over by a Reindeer." Today I heard it twice. My Pandora traditional Christmas station keeps things exciting.

It's also one of the big concert seasons for school choirs and bands at every level. In my grade, it's a time to show off the talent hiding effectively in the early elementary grades. The drill works like this. Impossibly cute little kids memorize lines that most parents are secretly hoping for them to mess up. The cutting room floor at *America's Funniest Home Videos* is littered with these "can't miss" entries. It's just a fun season all around.

On some of these days, we teachers get some work done. Yesterday was one of them. In exchange for a morning of sight words and hard and soft "G" sounds, I promised we'd listen to and learn a Donny Hathaway tune for Christmas. My babies worked their brains out. For those that don't know, Donny Hathaway is one that can bring a soulful sound to any song, and I mean any! There are not enough "O"s in smooth to describe him. He wrote "This Christmas" (the 30th most-performed holiday tune ever). We were going to learn that song and act it out.

When I hit the play button, I knew I had them. They were into it. What they didn't have in substance, they made up for in style. James, the best reader in class, always knew the next word in the lyric and was loud and not constrained by tune or pitch. Those who could hear him (including anyone within a city block) followed his lead. Like James, they sang off-key and gyrated in all kinds of directions, but importantly, they were loud and proud. But I must tell you, the most precious was when the quiet kid with a million-dollar smile on the front row finally found his inner Johnny Mathis.

The kid killed it. Honest to goodness, it gave me goose-bumps. For those unfamiliar with educational terms, that's our jargon for one of the most reliable metrics of good teaching. No, I didn't video their spirited performance for grown-up entertainment. I'm just not that kind of teacher. However, I do think I could take this crew on the road. We'd be available for all parties, baby showers, parades, supermarket openings, and any other special occasions any time after "The 12th of Never." You can reach us at 1-800-WESINGLOUD, extension, OFFKEY. This is a talented bunch, but "Chances Are" you knew that.

December 11

It's Hard to be Cool When You Smell Like Vicks

Teaching is a glamorous occupation.

My College Advisor

This Tuesday morning started with such purpose and noble intentions. Version A of the lesson plan on my desk laid out a clear path to valuable things a kid needs to know. However, before lunch, my children and I learned some good lessons on personal hygiene that, to my surprise, were not on the lesson plan, at least not that version.

The morning was clear and cold outside. It was warm enough inside my brightly decorated room, but an ill wind was sweeping across rows of tiny desks without my permission. Even old George Washington on the bulletin board was looking a bit peaked. One of my toughest kids, Henry, was sniffling a little, and his usually bright eyes were at half-mast or what some would call "droopy-eyed." He was one of twenty-three students in my classroom when the bell rang that morning, but before we lined up for lunch, twelve had left with fevers.

The arithmetic left me with ten hearty souls and Henry, one empty can of Lysol, one tube of Clorox Wipes smeared over anything that would stay still, twenty-two little hands full of sanitizer, and two teachers loading up on bright orange Vitamin C tablets. I remember thinking I would likely show up the next day with an orange tint to my skin. As my last line of defense, I got a blue jar of Vicks Vapor Rub out of my desk and practically covered my exposed body parts.

I'm not sure how effective this topical treatment is for getting me out of the singles ministry at church, but as Henry pointed out, I smelled like his grandpa's old cardigan. I think the medical rationale for that ointment is that all living things, including a virus, can't stand the smell. I promised my students that Vicks would not be my signature perfume this year. Henry seemed pleased. He told me so right before he checked out after lunch.

December 13

Days Before Christmas Break are Longer

Much that I sought, I could not find.

Much that I found I could not bind.

Much that I bound, I could not free.

But all that I freed came back to me.

Lee Wilson Todd

On most days, life is composed of a series of planned and unplanned moments that, when added up, the whole is usually equal to more than the sum of its parts. On days like today that bracket big holidays, this kind of arithmetic is as irrational as floaties on a flounder. On these days, 2+2=17.

Today it was hard to make sense of anything, but I've learned that even in the throes of a wild series of moments, something can happen that seems to tie it all together, at least for somebody. Sometimes, the only thing left to do is surrender to the moment. Follow fate's lead. Today was a good example.

I spent the better part of this morning refreshing my

students on good line etiquette and how to walk down the hall in a reasonably straight line. With my best examples still ringing in their tiny ears, I turned around on the way to lunch, hoping to see a military-style straight line. What I saw were a few kids doing something akin to yoga. Some were staring off into space (somewhere around Pluto), while others seemed to be auditioning a few ballet moves for a spot in our local production of *The Nutcracker.*

With a few line corrections and some scattered "Yes ma'am's," we finally got to the cafeteria. For some reason, Seth, who never gets into trouble, decided to scream a season's greeting to one of his buddies in Mrs. Miller's class sitting on the other side of the room. Why? "Just because."

Polite little Julie thought it would be nice if we had a little snowstorm to get us all in the spirit of the season. Without a forecast, she crumbled up her stale breadstick and tossed it into the air. Clearly, the cafeteria manager was not impressed with her meteorology skills nor with Bentley's guess that his milk, which was also white, might add to the festive occasion if it was freed from its box.

I marched right over and insisted that these two little part-time Oscar winners clean up the mess. The only sound then was a couple of muffled "yes ma'am's."

We finally got back to the class. With a few expert light

switch maneuvers, I finally got their attention for the afternoon lesson on subtraction that seemed so tight last night. Sabastian was sitting in the front row, my go-to math whiz who could probably teach the lesson should I be raptured. He was the first one I called on after asking, "If I had nine oranges and gave Sarah two, how many oranges would I have left?" With a grin that would stop a train, he shouted out loudly, "Twenty-three!" Even Jake, who had drifted off for his afternoon nap, thought that was hilarious.

I couldn't hold my laughter any longer. I lost it as I joined Liam, Jake, and the rest of their audience in a satisfying belly laugh that lasted a good five minutes. With Christmas break still five days away, we were kicking off this celebration of this season of "great joy" and "goodwill." Although I felt out of control most of the day, as it turned out, I learned a lot today. Merry Christmas!

January 7

Maybe God Wanted Me to Have a Snow Day

---

*"Let It Snow, Let It Snow,
Let It Snow."*

Julie Styne and Sammy Cahn

We all survived Christmas break and started school last Wednesday. We're now about three days into the new semester, and it's a little after nine on a Monday morning, and I'm still in my footed Zebra PJs, staring out the window and sipping hot chocolate from my favorite mug. One could argue I'm standing here because tiny seeds of faith were planted last Friday.

When school cranked back up last week, we were all settling in for that long stretch between Christmas break and Spring Break when the cold weather zaps most of our enthusiasm. To help acclimate the kids, we all decided to spend a few days talking about what we can look forward to since Big T's Snow Cone Shack is boarded up.

Winter's short dark stubby days are not glamourous and tend to slurp up the last bits of Christmas cheer and enthusiasm left in the human spirit. Like a PR agent, I was desperately trying to lighten the mood without a lot of success by pitching a lesson on winter fun. About the only thing winter has going for it is the soft white stuff that falls out of the sky and turns backyards into magical places, especially if they're hilly. Otherwise, the cold, damp, battleship gray days of winter seem to be the season of our collective discontent.

Consequently, the kindergarten teachers at my school decided we would sell winter by emphasizing all the fun things about snow. Of course, there were lots of snowman ideas, snow stories, snow plays, paper sculptures of snow, and snow sledding. "Snow" kidding, the ideas poured out like Morton's salt. Leaving that meeting, I could almost feel it snowing inside.

I tried out some of these ideas with my little people on Friday, and it was way more fun than any of us had planned. The skies were a dull lead color outside, but it felt bright and sunny inside. Gretchen, who had moved from western Pennsylvania, regaled the kids with tales of snowdrifts as high as our school windows. She had her classmates' attention. However, when she mentioned in passing that the drifts were so high that they had to call off school, they were lapping up her story like hungry hounds. She added, "You could play outside in it and not get dirty, plus we didn't have to go to school on snow days." At that point, you could see nineteen tiny mouths forming the word, "Wow!"

The rest of Friday afternoon was a discussion of how and why snowfalls and, of course, the big question, "How can we *make* it snow?" The only answer I had besides some odds and ends about fronts I had picked up from Channel 11's weatherman was, have faith. I was half kidding, but they were as serious as Michael Jordan's hairstylist.

I explained that faith, as one ancient writer put it, "is the substance of things hoped for..." (Hebrews 11:1). So, we decided to test that hypothesis over the weekend. Twenty little snow angels and I planted a tiny seed of faith on the way out of the door Friday. We told each other, "I'll see you Tuesday. Monday will be a snow day." Perhaps that's why I'm in my PJs this morning. But on the other hand, I'm still single.

Penguins are Odd and Even

"I Go for Penguins"

Lyle Lovett

We all have preferences, and thankfully, those differences make a big difference. Otherwise, we would all like Smokey Robinson, cringe at the sight of liver pudding, and wish that it would snow every day in the winter, but that's just me. In my experience, the tendency to prefer one thing over another is not limited to music, food, or changes in the weather. It seems to impact every aspect of our lives. For all of us to live together in relative peace and harmony, we must learn tolerance for those whose varied tastes in clothes, choice, and behavior tend to run counter to the crowd.

Ever since we began writing our stories down, great literature has tried to teach us (with mixed results) about acceptance, patience, and kindness in our treatment of each other. Without these guidelines, we revert to serious games of us and them, the default human position of destructive tribalism. That idea is worth discussing in graduate school seminars and classrooms where kids sit cross-legged on the floor while the teacher tries her best to sit in a chair designed for someone other than themselves.

The "great literature" I've chosen to begin this conversation with kids who can't stay inside the lines is Helen Lester's *Tacky the Penguin*. It's a story of Tacky, an odd penguin who stood out from the crowd, was often a little too loud, dressed funny, and did cannonball dives. He was on his own, over the top, and quite a funny bird. Most of us know a Tacky. The movie *Happy Feet* sparked a love for penguins like I've never known, especially for Tacky. This morning it was no problem getting the students to listen to the penguin's adventures that seemed so different.

As I read, we took frequent opportunities to discuss the meaning of the word odd and its implications. They were into it and seemed to get it that this likable odd bird was not an ordinary penguin. It felt like we were all coming to the point that maybe all penguins were not the same after all.

It felt like an appropriate time to check for understanding, so I said, "Children, let's review. Tacky was…" and left an appropriate blank for the kids to fill in. I fully expected to hear the word odd or maybe "different." Instead, the first and loudest student, of course, it was Jasmine, responded, "Tacky was cray cray!" Ummmmmmm! That possible response was not in my lesson plan. Perhaps Piaget was right. Little kids may not yet be ready for the grown-up lesson I learned today. Today, I taught myself.

January 15 and 16

Sometimes a Borrowed Dream Can Get You By

We hold these truths to be self-evident, that all men are created equal...

Thomas Jefferson

Yesterday was special. Over the last two days, we have celebrated a hero to almost everybody, Dr. Martin Luther King. His name is familiar to most students, primarily as a central freeway in town. Though they may know that he is the reason there is no school on Monday, they are not as clued in on what his contributions were or why we celebrated his birthday. I know because I asked them to write about it. One of my better writers, Alex, summed it up with a line or two. He said, "Dr. King had a speech. He was trying to be nice. It was called *I Have a Dream.*"

What he didn't say that most of us know by heart is that dreams can change lives. Most of my students are African American and are politely labeled "at-risk" due to several factors. In most cases, it results from poverty's grip on their young lives. It has choked out most of their families' dreams and, by extension, their own. It's difficult to dream about tomorrow if today there's a real question about what I'll eat tonight and where we will move next month. Too often, dreams are luxuries of those who have a well-stocked pantry and are current on the rent. Children are natural sponges and quickly absorb the bitter realities their caregivers wrestle with every day. Poverty and its cousin racism crush too many dreams, especially the tiny green shoots that tend to spring up naturally in a *kinder* garden.

To see a man stand up against his oppressors in the face of overwhelming odds is a powerful lesson that endures and one that should be celebrated. Dr. King, who looks like most of my students, stood in our nation's capital and confidently declared...

> In a sense, we've come to our nation's capital to cash a check. When the architects of our republic wrote the magnificent words of the Constitution and the Declaration of Independence, they were signing a promissory note to which every American was to fall heir. This note was a promise that all men, yes, black men as well as white men, would be guaranteed the unalienable rights of life, liberty, and the pursuit of happiness... We can never be satisfied as long as our children are stripped of their selfhood and robbed of their dignity...I have a dream that my four little children will one day live in a nation where they will not be judged by the

color of their skin but by the content of their character. I have a dream today (Martin Luther King, Jr., August 28, 1963, Washington, DC.).

Regardless of race, color, creed, or national origin, the dream still reverberates across this country. Perhaps his legacy is that his dream can be checked out of the library and downloaded into tiny hearts and minds with powerful implications. Sometimes a borrowed dream is all it takes to change the trajectory of a life. The possibility of enriching a life is something to celebrate. Besides, it's nice to help others.

February 9

You Can Learn Stuff in the Age of Puddles

I wanted to be a teacher when I grow up, but my first name isn't Mrs.

An Anonymous 5-year-old

I've learned a lot listening to kids. However, paying attention to children is a lot of tough work. Although I work in a learning-rich environment, I admit that I've strongly considered that truck driving school in Raleigh on a few bad days. It can sometimes take a few days of serious reflection on what was said and not said, but I've found that listening is a powerful learning tool.

Some of the scraps of wisdom I've picked up from my students have been funny, a few profound, and some simply absurd, at least in the first hearing. I have found that giving their ideas a second thought (sometimes it takes a third or fourth) has nurtured my thinking and learning.

Today it happened during a rather innocent conversation with one of my students about a book she and her grandma (mostly grandma) were reading. With the excitement usually reserved for recess, Nicole stood at the corner of my desk, fiddling with her braids as I finished some paperwork.

When I looked up, she said, "Ms. Hardaway, me and my grandma are reading a book about puddles and ponds and how they are alike and different!"

"Puddles and ponds?" I asked incredulously. I could see she heard my skepticism and wanted desperately to tell me more. As the ideas tumbled in her head, it was evident she was trying to fit them into words so she could share her new insights with me.

Unfortunately, at the time, I was still stuck on puddles and ponds and how they could be *that* interesting. I furrowed my brow and could only manage a blank, vacant stare. However, I did have a semester or two of elementary methods and quickly recovered with an invitation for more information. Right out of the textbook, I said, "Tell me more about how ponds and puddles are like you and how they are different."

She looked at me as if I had just fallen off the turnip truck and said, "A puddle is brown like you and me and my grandma." I was amazed and more than a little confused. After all, this profound statement came from somebody not as old as my car.

Once again, I asked the standard follow-up question, "Why?" The little teacher, unwilling to embarrass me, leaned in and whispered, "It's brown because it has mud in it." I could only manage another long "ummmmmm…" and mumbled, "Interesting."

I don't know if I was shocked or disturbed or just plain surprised. I decided not to get too deep in the weeds of self-image and ethnicity, so I shifted gears and probed another line of reasoning. "How are puddles and ponds like each other?"

This time with an eye roll as if she were mortified at my ignorance, she put her hands on her hips. Emphasizing each word in the sentence, she announced, "They're the same age. Puddles and ponds are the same!" Can you say blank stare? Can you say slow blink? Happy Thursday.

The Last Bell is the Saddest

Any man's death diminishes me,
because I am involved in mankind...

John Donne
Devotions Upon Emergent Occasions,
Meditation XVII

John Donne, the old pastor at Saint Paul's in London, knew that we are all intimately wound together, that "No man is an island, entirely unto himself." Perhaps more than any other profession, teachers know the sheer delight of watching children succeed and the utter heartbreak of witnessing their failure. We belong to each other. Their successes and failures matter to me. This is *our* class.

For good teachers, that bond lasts as long as either of the parties is alive. My elementary teachers are still walking the halls of my brain, even after some have passed. I could tell that Mrs. Hall, my high school English teacher, liked me, even though she made it seem like she didn't like anyone in my class. I can still hear her voice in the middle of Walmart even though she died years ago. She still hassles me about my manners, spelling, and making sure that I express my opinions clearly. Good teaching lasts far beyond the last bell.

Now that I'm on Mrs. Hall's side of the teacher's desk, I've learned some painful lessons about my Teacher-Mommy role. I found out today that one of my former students I had as a fifth-grader years ago died. There's nothing enjoyable about reading obituaries of a young man that once drew your picture with fat crayons or whom you've talked strongly to about potential. I clearly remember days of him smiling and being silly. Seeing his characteristic wry smile in an obituary picture and reading the word death in the following writing broke my heart. There are persistent troubling questions—did I encourage him enough? Did I point him in the right direction? Did I do my best? I think so, but it's so heartbreakingly sad!

I tell my students and their parents that once they're mine, they will always be my children. Always! I just ran into one of my "daughters." She's a young mommy now, and some of life's rough cords have rubbed her soul raw. I truly wish things were different for her, but I gave her all I had. She said she was just talking about me the other day, and we shared a few laughs.

Even though things have not worked out for her, I have no regrets. I have chosen this occupation that demands that every day I give away the gifts Mrs. Hall gave me—even with all my imperfections, I mattered. Inspired by her confidence in me, I have tried to teach "wide open." Although it's not spelled out in my contract, I do love my babies hard. I'm all in. No matter the circumstance, that bond never ends with the last bell, no matter how sad.

There Are Sore Winners

If you hold a cat by the tail, you learn things you cannot learn any other way.

Mark Twain

It was a beautiful spring day, so I decided we'd all go outside and enjoy the sunshine and a good game of kickball. I slipped on the old Nikes that I keep in my desk for emergency purposes and joined an eager bunch of little people on the playground.

When it was over, I felt like the ball. I think my students beat me up today on purpose. I don't know if it was because I looked like a Bobo doll or the kids had been cooped up too long, but I will need a tub of *Icy Hot* when I get home. I bruise easier than a five-day-old banana.

Along with the good-natured roughhousing, we had a little drama brewing at second base. Lisa, who was firmly planted on second, "That's the way you 'pose' to play it," she said, would not share it with Edward, who had kicked a double. I knew this wouldn't end well, so I shifted gears and decided we'd have a few races. I thought a good foot race would burn off some steam and excess energy. All I would have to do is be the finish line and the timing judge. None of that required movement. What could go wrong?

Plenty, as it turns out. I stood on one end of the field, and my little track stars about forty yards away. In pairs, they would start when I dropped my hand and then race to me, and I would give them a time.

I never said, "When you get to me, tag me." Somehow, that became the thing to do. Each group racing toward me would tag me like they were barreling into second base on a close call. The cumulative effect of repeated tags from those tiny hands hurt. A few boys took advantage of the situation and punched the big Bobo doll. I knew it had gotten out of hand when one of my boys forgot about the race and just stood there, hitting me and laughing. My only defense was what professional fighters would call a clinch. Like Sugar Ray, I hugged the little guy, and we both laughed. Friends, that was an "old school" fun day on the playground, painful but fun. Speaking of old school, I think I need to add a little *Epsom Salts* to my well-deserved hot bath this evening.

My Best is Good Enough

Simplify, simplify, simplify.

Henry David Thoreau, in Walden

Teacher Appreciation Week and Christmas are two of the main times that teachers have the wonderful experience of opening gifts from students and parents that express their gratitude and love. I try my best to make sure that I take the time to open each gift with the student so that they can experience, firsthand, the joy and excitement I have for them and their efforts to bless my life.

There is one type of gift that will ensure that a teacher's heart will smile so loud. That is that unexpected homemade gift that you know was made with nothing but pure love. Like all teachers, I love gifts and appreciate the thoughts behind them, but gifts, like love, are best when they are "homemade." No matter how inexpensive the material looks, it means so much more when our friends, family, and students take the time to make the present personally. As corny as it sounds, both the thoughts behind the time and effort count. Sure, I like fine, expensive things, but I don't need them, especially from my students.

The educational opportunity I offer them is mostly homemade with my time and effort as the raw materials. Like most homemade things, a good education is never perfect or finished. There is always some assembly required, and it generally takes a lifetime to complete—neither *Walmart* nor the *Dollar Store* stocks a decent off-the-shelf education. To paraphrase the Beatles, the education you take is equal to the education you make.

Consequently, it was such a welcomed surprise today when cute little Denise, grinning from ear to ear, brought in a small cardboard box with a dirty pink ribbon tied around it in a tight knot. Judging from the package, it was clearly homemade. I couldn't wait to open it.

As excited as I was to tear into it, Denise seemed twice as excited to be giving it. The look on her face was priceless. With absolutely no self-consciousness about her missing two front teeth and the tendency for her tongue to find the gap, she proudly declared, "Myth Hardaway, ith for you. I made it my thelf."

Before I even looked in the box, I knew I'd treasure it forever, but more importantly, I felt deeply loved. Inside the box was a small herd of lovingly used plastic ponies that she decorated in various colors with what looked like leftover paint and a little glitter for effect. Last week she mentioned that she liked horses, and I automatically said, "Me too."

As one old itinerate preacher entering a church once told the man begging at the door, "silver and gold have I none, but such as I have, give I thee" (Acts 3:6).

Priceless.

April 13

" ... A Little Child Shall Lead Them."

Isaiah 11:6

Tomorrow is Earth Day, and we are gearing up for it. We're learning a great deal about this beautiful, fascinating, unique, amazing planet called Earth. In preparation, we've been taking *YouTube* field trips around the world. All this free travel has blessed my life, and I hope it expanded my students' understanding of what lies just beyond the horizon.

Every time we look at a new place or see interesting plants or animals, we talk about what we can do to keep it beautiful and fresh. In our discussions of recycling and littering, we also talked about a new word, pollution. My kids are now firm believers in making the Earth healthy and not sick.

At recess today, one of my little girls ran to me quite excited with a piece of paper, breathlessly yelling, "Miss Hardaway, Miss Hardaway, I found pollution!"

Driving home today, it occurred to me that maybe it's time to bring back the old trash commercial featuring a proud, teary-eyed Native American. We're drowning in pollution. Tomorrow, I'll say a lot more about it.

Be Kind to Your Mother

Leave things like you found them.

Mama (Janice Hardaway)

O ne of the joys I have of being a teacher is that I have the wonderful opportunity of laying the foundation for what my students may come to love and appreciate. Fortunately, or unfortunately, I teach them from what I have been personally exposed to, and those experiences are filtered through my brain and are consequently uniquely interpreted. As you have no doubt noticed, sometimes—as the carpenters would say—I'm about a half a bubble off level. And those may be my better days.

For teachers, the school days around special days like Earth Day or Easter break provide good examples of how thinking gets creative. Taking advantage of these teachable moments is what we do and what most often sticks in the tiny brains and occasionally in the economy-sized ones.

On these days, for good or ill, I am their tour guide through magical lands that exist somewhere out there beyond where the sidewalk ends. Most of my children hear for the first time about exotic, strange customs in faraway places as I interpret them and see events as I describe them. These days are fun and are easy targets for a creative teacher. Towels transform into turbans, dirt piles become pyramids, and almost any teacher can do the elephant trunk trick, complete with the sound.

Today, we are celebrating Earth Day, and as I tried to explain, the world on this side of the sidewalk is just as exotic as Timbuktu if you look close enough. What happens here really matters. This is our neighborhood. My goal was to have them develop a deep appreciation for the fragile blue ball we all call home. Although a clever *YouTube* clip is only a couple of clicks away, I would rather give them a hands-on experience in loving Mother Earth and enjoying all the good things that come with a healthy relationship with her.

The basic rules of how we ought to behave toward her were written by Robert Fulghum back in the late 1980s. Quoting from what could easily be our class rules, he suggested,

> Share everything. Play fair...Don't hit people. Put things back where you found them. Clean up your own mess. Don't take things that aren't yours. Say you are sorry when you hurt somebody. Wash your hands before you eat. Flush...Take a nap every afternoon. When you

go out into the world, watch for traffic, hold hands, and stick together. Be aware of wonder...And it is still true, no matter how old you are when you go out into the world, it is best to hold hands and stick together.
(Robert Fulghum, 1989, All I Needed to Know I Learned in Kindergarten)

Amen, Brother Fulghum! No one could say it better, but these are words. For my children, passive strings of letters are not as powerful as actually *doing* "Earth Day" things. So, we decided on a picnic with food directly from Mother Earth or as close as we could get. We banned food in decorated Styrofoam containers and anything with a catchy commercial tagline. We had cucumbers, carrots, celery sticks, and a healthy bottle of water.

Then I introduced hummus. That day we ate from the Earth, and most learned a new word as foreign as Timbuktu. It was not a stretch for them to pick up on the skills needed to eat food with their hands, but the hummus was a difficult sell. They were clueless about how to eat it until I demonstrated the technique with a few Wheat Thins. It was a good excuse to lick our fingers. A few liked the hummus, but most of them reacted as if I was teaching a lesson on algebra. Lots of blank stares, and only one turned green, but of course, it was Earth Day.

An Imagination on Fire Can be Dangerous

ANYTHING can happen child,

ANYTHING can be.

Shel Silverstein
Where the Sidewalk Ends

Teachers are dangerous people—at least the good ones are. They set fires to tender imaginations, then sit back and watch them burn right through a string of thinking rules. For these little people, truly, anything is possible.

As most teachers have noticed, the typical number two pencil can be a drumstick tapping out annoying sounds, but in NASCAR country and Robert's front jean pocket, it was a cool gear shift for his sporty little two-footed midget racer. I know because I had to flip on the caution light as he shifted down around the corner of my desk. I heard the *eeeeeek* of his squealing tires as his breaks locked up in turn four as he crashed into the trash can.

For my children, the world is more of a playground of

possibilities than an oyster. It is something to be relished, enjoyed, and celebrated. Some of them hum as they work. For others, everything they touch is some kind of musical instrument. I've seen desk sets that double as spelling books, broomsticks become guitars, and trumpets that look suspiciously like rulers. Often, I'm treated to impromptu concerts, usually accompanied by an interpretative dance.

In the hands of such children, a single crayon can be an instrument that beautifully expresses sheer joy without words. Housekeeping can be set up between the monkey bars and the swings on the playground. Problems are created and resolved in these playhouses, often without breaking a sweat.

I've also watched as children on the playground are mesmerized by an ant colony and captivated by the tiny rolly pollies that share our space. As these little artists, sociologists, and biologists know, there are many fascinating things to learn and places to explore everywhere—especially if you play hard enough. To an imagination on fire, "anything is possible...anything can be." I have to go. I think I smell smoke.

April 26

The Sun Shines Even on Cloudy Days

---

*"Some Days Are Diamonds
(Some Days Are Stone)"*

*Performed by John Denver
written by Dick Feller*

For many reasons, a few days are better known than others; some days are just better. Some days sparkle, and every now and then, the day can be cold, lifeless, and just plain hard. On these days, an invocation of a higher power is necessary to get to the dismissal bell and survive my turn at bus duty. So, today's ditty will be a short prayer I wrote that I've learned to lean on several times. It might fit you. Feel free to use it but add your name at the end. I'd hate to get the Lord confused.

Dear Lord, you are the Creator of us all and clearly in charge of everything, including the weather conditions. I know you probably already have weather fronts scheduled, but could you possibly hold off the rain today until after recess? These short, loud people (you know who I'm talking about) need to run around and scream a little; otherwise, I will. We'd do all of that in here, but

I'm afraid my principal wouldn't get it (again, you know who I'm talking about).

Father, their whisper voice has modulated up to eleven, and I'm a bit frazzled. However, I understand that you have other things to attend to, like hard-headed politicians, greedy bankers, and some needy folks in Africa, not to mention the thirsty flowers and plants around here that could be crying out even louder than me. I also understand, as it is commonly said, that "April showers bring May flowers."

I get all of that, but I'm desperate. So please redirect the heavy clouds I'm watching out my window toward our surrounding farms where they'd be welcomed. Like me, farmers need a break now and again too. As you know, it's getting on toward the end of the year, and my kids are restless and need to get out in the sunshine and act their age. I have little to bargain with, but as I said, you know who I'm talking about.

Amen!

PS. Please do something nice for the elementary teachers in Seattle. I hear it rains a lot out there.

Love, Vanessa

May 3

Kindergarten Should Not
be a Tinder Moment

---

*If you were a vegetable, you'd be a
"cute cumber."*

A Cheesy Pick-Up Line

L ife is simple from a child's perspective. If he wants it, he asks for it. If he thinks it, he says it. There are no big, fancy words, no thinking, and no beating around the bush. In some ways, that's an admirable way to live in this grown-up world. But there are always boundaries and hard realities. Children are generally unaware of the social contract that permits some things and limits others. That's especially so in loving relationships and a lesson that must be taught and learned. We shirk this responsibility at our own peril.

In my world, a little boy watches a little girl two tables over. He is captivated by how she uses her fat red pencil, organizes her crayons in alphabetical order, and the amazing way she colors inside the lines. In various forms, love happens everywhere, including a kindergarten class. Although Jalen didn't know him, the early 20th-century American philosopher William James who wrote "Feelings are facts," would have understood what our young Lothario had to do.

Confidently, the little five-year-old Jalen sashayed over to her table and promptly proposed to the little girl with the alphabetical crayons. Surprisingly, she turned him down, and it was not the first time. After a little investigation, I found out this was not his first proposal. The kid is persistent. Ultimately, it may have been her captivating beauty that got to him. Apparently, there's something about a couple of missing front teeth that he found attractive.

This baby wanted my teacher's assistant and me to know that he did not appreciate our interruption of this one-sided tender moment for reasons obvious to you and me (but not him). He was incensed that I intervened in his romantic mission. This whole whacky episode got me thinking of absurd possibilities. If this is what being a kindergarten teacher is all about, should I set up a series of *Singles Kinder-Conferences* to accommodate these tiny miniature humans? If so, here might be some ideas for breakout sessions at my school conference in the backroom at *Chucky Cheese*:

- Playground Proposals: It's All in Your Words
- Just Because He Can Color in the Lines Does Not Make Him Spouse Material
- He Shared His Chips with Another Girl: Now What?
- My Glue Ran Out, but He Gave Me His: Is He the

One?

- Snickers are not Always Sweet

Registration information coming soon. Get your mom and dad to read it to you.

Here I sit, learning lessons from a five-year-old on how to come out of the singles ministry. These people have no jobs, no vehicles, but already know how to sweep someone off their feet! Now that is a tender and sweet moment. Let's hang on to the hope that such a conference is never necessary.

These boys and girls are inundated with sex on a variety of social media platforms. Some of the little people say and suggest things that are way out of bounds. Although they may be learning from their slightly older siblings that sex is a plaything—another toy to replace the Tonka truck—most of us know it's not. They don't.

For my money, our babies are starting way too early. Kindergarten should not be a "Tinder Moment." Anyway, "Tinder" is not even spelled right.

May 5

When School's Over Education Begins

---

*Today you are you. / That is truer
than true. / There is no one alive /
who is youer than you.*

Dr. Suess

It is teacher appreciation week, and I've been thinking a lot about what I've chosen to do with my life and what difference that choice has made. I expect I'll get a few cards this week from my current crop of little humans and maybe a box of chocolate-covered cherries or a fragrance or two that begins with, "If you like...." Please don't think I'm complaining. I am truly grateful, but I don't do this job for the gratuities no matter the costs. Besides, as I wrote earlier, I enjoy homemade stuff.

This is a serious job that should make a difference for both teachers and learners. I can confidently report that this profession, the hundreds of children I've taught, and their families have certainly made a difference in my life. Obviously, I can't say that's true for every child on the "learning side" of my desk over the last two decades. However, recently, I have been reminded of how my career choice has intersected in meaningful ways with at least two former students and their families.

The first happened last week. A former student's mom informed me that her daughter was having issues with being brown. Having some experience with that situation and a long history with this child, I knew I had to get involved. She was still "my child" and just two halls away, so I asked her to drop by my room after school.

That afternoon, she walked into my room with no hint of a smile of recognition, her head was bowed, and she made little to no eye contact. It was clear that this little girl was struggling. Her identity issues seem to have eroded any sense of self-confidence and threatened her well-being. Undeterred, I plowed straight into the problem.

I held her hands and talked about how God loves color, how He splashed it all over our world. If you'll notice, the Creator used every color in his big box of Crayola's. He daubed it on lilies and leaves, chameleons and caterpillars, and horses and hounds. For his human creation, he used a lot of different earth tones.

He mixed them all on a big artist pallet, and now we are all kinds of tints and shades, hues, and colors. Each one of us is the artist's personal and unique creation. As crazy as it sounds, each of us is His personal favorite. I took her tiny hand and pointed out the little squiggly lines on the end of her fingers. "See, this is where God personally signed you. This signature is unlike any other person in the world. You are a one-of-a-kind art piece."

How much of this sunk in, I don't know. But I did notice the beginnings of a smile at the corners of her mouth. We compared our fingerprints then we put our arms side by side. We talked about how her "brown" and my "brown" are slightly different, though they looked similar at first. We then counted the number of fingers dangling off the end of each of our hands and arrived at the same number. We were a lot alike.

Though the arithmetic matched, as we looked closer, we found subtle differences in our arms in tint and tone and size and shape. We joked, at least I did, about the differences. As we moved our fingers, we talked about how amazing that complicated, simple-looking task was and the intelligent design that went into this act that most of us take for granted. We concluded that God does all things well! Then I reminded her that the one who could do all of this does not make junk. Now we were both laughing.

The second chance to be "an instrument of God's peace" was the product of a recent conversation with one of my high school teacher colleagues. She was telling me about one of my former students who was struggling. She knew we were close, although it had been about a decade since he had colored in my class. He was having issues with the consequences of poor decisions. His choices could easily bend the arc of his life in a bad direction.

His story is all too familiar. As a child of poverty, the lure of easy, fast money was too tempting. The burden of *helping* his single mom was noble, but I knew that neither she nor her son could live with the method. He was beginning to bet his freedom and maybe his life on a bunch of faulty premises that were sketchy. It was clear to all of us that he knew better.

He was almost grown, but he was not too big for me to insist he come to my kindergarten classroom. The mothering instinct in lower elementary teachers is not confined to the current school year. We sat down around the same tiny tables where he had learned to stay in the lines not many years ago.

I reached across the table and took his hands in mine. Staring him down and without a smile, I launched into my blistering sermon on decision making. I hit every mark, from brushing teeth to choice of friends and the consequences involved in all of it. About halfway into it, I noticed his eyes were getting a little leaky. I poured it on a little more, then downshifted to a slower pace and a softer tone. After a few minutes, we planned for him to check back with me in a week to let me know how things were going. We hugged and made promises that I hope he keeps—especially those on the dental hygiene issues.

So, in this teacher appreciation week, I'm grateful that my babies love me and that I truly love them, all of them, forever. I am also thankful that even when they are too big to sit in the tiny chairs, they freely come back and try. I am most grateful that my opportunity to teach and learn is not hemmed in by the rhythm of a school year. As I've discovered in so many ways, when school's over, the education begins.

Kids Say the Smartest Things

---

*I was ugwee at the doctor, now I
won't get a tweet.*

*Josie, 3
My niece crying after an
un-lady like doctor's visit*

A few decades back in TV history, Art Linkletter had a *House Party* and always invited little kids over to talk about stuff. Unencumbered by the restrictions of social correctness and adultish reasoning, these free-thinking kids unloaded on various topics. Their wit and wisdom were collected in Linkletter's book, *Kids Say the Darndest Things.* He listened to their take on a range of issues from romance, "Always tell your girlfriend she looks nice, even if she looks like a truck" (James, age 8), to daily showers, "My hair is so long because I water it every day" (Jenny, age 7).

A first-grade teacher asked children to reflect on common advice that adults use to encourage, cajole, and teach others. These kids were given the first part of the advice and asked to complete it to make sense, at least to them. Their take on the so-called wisdom of "big people" is clearly more direct and often sometimes more reasonable than the original old worn-out phrases we've thrown around with virtually no thought. Here's a sample:

- Don't change horses...............*until they stop running.*
- You can lead a horse to water, but.....................*how?*
- Don't bite the hand that............................*looks dirty.*
- The pen is mightier than...................................*the pig.*
- A miss is as good as a.. *mister.*
- You can't teach an old dog new...........................*math.*
- If you lie down with dogs, you'll...............*stink in the morning.*
- Where there's smoke, there's....................... *pollution.*
- A penny saved is...*not much.*
- Don't put off till tomorrow what.............. *you put on to go to bed.*
- Laugh, and the whole world laughs with you, cry, and...*you have to blow your nose.*
- Children should be seen and not.................. *spanked or grounded.*
- If at first, you don't succeed.......... *get new batteries.*
- You get out of something only what you... *see in the picture on the box.*
- When the blind lead the blind.... *get out of the way.*

Young eyes tend to see things for what they are, no more and no less. Children have a way of cutting through the cheap glass of our maturity and offering

111

us unrestricted fresh insights into how things are or maybe ought to be. They are easily awed by things we long ago dismissed as common and ordinary—specks of dust floating in the sunlight, the interesting way a caterpillar gets around, and the sound the air conditioner makes.

A note I got today from a fat red pencil reminded me of their gifts and insights. It read, "The Earth is beautiful because it has butterflies. The Earth is beautiful because it has flowers. The Earth is beautiful because it has birds. The Earth has dogs."

No wonder the Creator urged us "to become as little children...." If we headed His advice, I think we'd have a lot more fun and a lot fewer doctor bills.

May 25

Big Choices are Often Made in Tiny Chairs

The place God calls you to is the place where your deep gladness and the world's deep hunger meet.

Fredrick Buechner
Wishful Thinking

Yesterday, I was in the grocery store and ran into Ms. Gloria Henderson. She was one of those "dangerous teachers" I wrote about earlier (see April 21). Ms. Henderson was one of my father's colleagues back in the day. A few years later, she put a match to my imagination. She was my father's friend, and I am honored to be sitting here writing about both of these giants in my educational history.

Like good teachers everywhere, she remembers my family. She had to because I sat in her 7th-grade class. Without even looking at the tea leaves at the bottom of my *Boys II Men* teacup, Ms. Henderson told me way back then that I would be a teacher, just like my daddy.

As I reflect on past conversations with her stretching back to grade school, I think she trained me to do what has brought me such "deep gladness" over the last few years. At the time, I thought we were just talking. However, like so many, I didn't listen as closely as I should have. As my preacher friends (my daddy chief among them) would say, I *ran* from my calling.

Like most teenagers, I thought I knew what I wanted, and it was certainly not in the "family business" at some elementary school. Stubbornly, I chose to major in business. I kind of liked the idea of making lots of money and making important decisions (at least one out of two). As I've realized, birds fly, fish swim, and Hardaways teach. I couldn't escape. I had chalk dust in my DNA.

Even with those vital clues about what I was intended to do, I graduated with my hard-earned business degree and went to work in a bank. It didn't take long for me to learn that banks do indeed have lots of money, but like some of my kids, they don't like to share. In my experience, people who are "*calling* fugitives" are not a happy bunch. They tend to use the word "stuck" a lot to describe their current position and rarely use terms like *joy, rewarding,* or *fulfilling* to describe how they make a living.

Fortunately, I found a local university that offered a degree that bridged the gap between my current work and teacher certification. In that program, I found other like-minded souls who were tired of running away from their *calling*. We bonded and helped each other through an intense and grueling graduate program that ended with teacher certification and lifelong friendships. Incidentally, as a bonus, I also picked up some handy tricks and tips that I still use in my classroom.

Eventually, I found a spot in an elementary school and settled in to try to do what Ms. Henderson and my Creator thought I *should*. Like my favorite teachers, I wanted to make a difference more than anything. Like them, I poured myself into my *calling* and, by extension, my students' lives.

It's still too early to judge the impact I've made, but there are some indicators that I'm doing what I was intended to do. Lea, one of my early kindergartners and now a beautiful young lady, graduated from high school last Saturday! In her time with me, she was the subject of a difficult custody battle between two loving adults. She was collateral damage in this family's domestic struggles and often turned to me for consolation. These tender moments left no doubt that I had chosen the right path.

More confirmation followed. Axel, a 5th-grade student, was the first family to invite me to dinner. It was a loud gathering punctuated by lots of laughter and highlighted by a delicious and authentic Puerto Rican dinner. It felt just like my family. This curious little boy is now a private pilot who makes a living solving real-world issues. So many others have now gone on to impressive careers and social success, and I'm so proud of each one.

If Ms. Henderson, at the urging of our Creator, had not interrupted my life with her direct and powerful guidance, I would not have known these young people who have so enriched my life. Like Ms. Henderson, the babies who sit in my little kindergarten class will never be too far away. In my heart, they will never outgrow their tiny chairs. These blubbering reflections are probably due to this time of year. I'll be saying goodbye to my current bunch soon, at least for now. However, my heart is full of gladness. I know deep down that our parting is just temporary.

A Plastic Dinosaur Can Cure What Ails You

My kingdom for a horse…

William Shakespeare
Richard III

Frank was proud of a Band-Aid his mom had used to cover a nasty cut on his elbow after a bike wreck. This morning I had to slip on my surgical gloves and perform a *bandaidectomy* (I just invented that word) after he had another run-in with the ground, aggravating the old injury. The old Band-Aid had to come off, and we had to have a new one. Apparently, running with scissors is not the only dangerous thing that can happen on the playground.

I took him inside to take care of the matter. According to five-year-old Frank, this new trauma made my Frank's blood pressure go up. His diagnosis was made without any troublesome medical equipment or a history of hypertension. Some things you just know.

He bravely fought back the tears, but I suppose that's normal for a kid with high blood pressure problems to face a complicated *bandaidectomy*. He proudly repeated his diagnosis, "My blood pressure is way up!" to everybody we passed on the way inside, and I mean everybody.

To calm him a little and get his blood pressure under control, I promised him a trip to the *Treat Box*. However, he had to be brave and remain calm throughout the impending high-class medical procedure (hey, I had real rubber gloves on) of removing one Band-Aid and replacing it with a fresh one.

I'm certainly not a doctor, but I think I witnessed a medical miracle this morning.

When we finished, I took Frank over to the *Treat Box*, and he picked out a cool red plastic T-Rex. Immediately, according to Frank, his blood pressure returned to normal before heading back outside to play. I learned that there must be some healing properties in either cheap plastic, dinosaurs, or both. I think I'll offer my colleague across the hall a trip to my *Treat Box*. Like Frank, she too suffers from "high blood pressure."

May 31

You Can Find Love in a Box of Crayons

Beauty in things exists merely in the mind which contemplates them.

David Hume
Essays, Moral and Political, 1742

Art is subjective. It can reveal a lot about the artist and sometimes provide an insight or two on the subject. As the subject of many kids' drawings, I've been drawn more times than Mona Lisa but rarely as flattering. These impressionistic art assignments are generally the result of the prompt, *My Teacher Is…*

This exercise lets me check in with my students and see how things are going. Drawing can be a non-threatening (at least to the students) opportunity to vent frustrations or express approval without words. As psychologists have taught us, there are things to learn in their choices involving colors, shapes, and included elements. They can reflect deeper feelings that are hard to put into words for any of us, especially a five-year-old.

Based on a sample of selected "art pieces" and my limited ability to analyze them, there are some rare dark-themed drawings, but most seem to be joyous expressions of contented school life. These effective statements about what's going on inside are without the constraint of cumbersome rules, proportion, gravity, and other basic laws of physics. As Picasso once said, "It took me a lifetime to learn to draw like a child."

The budding young artists that my colleagues and I sit for and teach tend to get the *number* of facial features about right—two eyes and two ears, one nose, and one mouth. The similarities end there. My eyes vary from dots to circles, and my nose is always interesting. Teacher mouths generally look like an Amazon logo, but sometimes, especially after an altercation, I have V-shaped teeth that look awfully menacing. There may be some kind of pent-up frustration there, and I bet Freud could make of lot out of it.

The point is that these little people offer me honest feedback when I am ready to "hear" it. After twenty years of looking at their art, it's clear to me that I'm not perfect. The one good thing that has resulted from this activity is a marked improvement in my personal prayer life.

When these young Leonardos enthusiastically show me their creations, usually my first reaction is something like, "Well, look at that." When I look closer at the grinning toothless artists and then at the drawing, I see things that people see in fancy art museums. I see hints at movement, balance, harmony, structure, and most of all, the artists' feelings.

For me, their artwork is special, representing, for the most part, wordless expressions of love. Smushed between crooked, out-of-place noses, scraggly mouth lines, and dotted eyes are the tender feelings a student has for her teacher. These short people are teaching me what college philosophy professors tried to do without a lot of success. I'm learning that real beauty is in the limitless power of the mind that contemplates it and in the understanding eye that soaks it in. I have lots of masterpieces to prove it.

June 1

Life is Filling in the Blanks

Plan, but plan in pencil.

*A reflection from a
student-teacher in Africa*

We are now into June, and the school year is wrapping up. To fill in the blanks between here and the actual last day of school, we are doing an exciting project that combines graphing and coloring, pretty heady concepts for most children. It involves locating a square box with certain coordinates and then coloring in that box with a specific color, a fresh take on the old paint by numbers activity. Some smart person figured out how little squares of blue and gray can be magically transformed into almost anything if the surrounding color squares are in the right place (my dad could make a sermon out of that, but I digress).

Earlier, I introduced this project and offered hints at the mystery picture that will emerge out of the confusion if we do it right. There seemed to be genuine excitement building, but it could have been the smell of fresh boxes of Crayola's. The kids worked hard and seemed to be in deep thought about locating the box on the grid that had to be magenta and only magenta. After all, rules are rules.

Amid this intense concentration, one of my sweet babies, whose group had just picked out the magenta coordinates, raised her hand. I was preparing for a question that would show off my fancy algebra graphing skills I learned in high school (or was supposed to). A little nervous, I said, "Yes, Janie?" Seriously, she shifted her brow as if bracing for the answer and asked, "Ms. Hardaway, is Kevin Hart dead?"

I was absolutely lost. Where did that come from? The only thing I had, was the teacher's stock answer, "I don't think so, but we'll find out." Great! Now I have to work on an episode of *Entertainment Tonight* between reviews of my 10th-grade algebra notes and the origins of the word "magenta." They told me the last few days of school might be the hardest.

June 8

Three R's Can Save Your Life

*The only thing that interferes with my
learning is my education.*

Albert Einstein

Yesterday was the last full day of school, and I'm exhausted. I'm physically drained and so full of raw human emotion that it's beginning to leak out of my eyes. As one old writer put it, "my cup running over."

Usually, my students and I spend the last day cleaning our room and laughing a lot. When we finish our chores, we throw a big party complete with lots of goodies that would mortify a dietitian, a bunch of silly games that would embarrass an account executive, and loads of pure, untainted fun.

We did all of that yesterday, but this morning I spent part of the day with one of mine in the Pediatric Unit of our local hospital. She's had some pretty rough and intense days, but I'm so grateful to report that her condition has gotten much better! I think most of that significant improvement is due to a ragged old teddy bear, praying relatives and teachers, lots of colorful misspelled cards, balloons, bubbles, and perhaps a little medical intervention—not necessarily in that order.

This morning in my car, between hospital visits and an early morning Walmart run for doughnuts and orange juice, I got a little choked up. I reflected on my "calling" and was so humbled by the opportunities it afforded me to make a difference this day. I was also overwhelmed by the encouragement and support of my professional colleagues over the last few weeks. Today was another affirmation that what we do is more than a *job*. I think I now know what it was that drew my daddy—the most compassionate man I know—to the crazy, wonderful way to make a living and a life. What an honor to be in a profession that nurtures learning, embraces change, and celebrates real life at every age, every day, everywhere.

I've learned and tried to teach my children that gratefulness is a better motivator than a set of Tony Robbins tapes. Consequently, I was pumped and ready by the time I got back to the classroom. As our morning breakfast celebration was winding down, it was time to get serious. Frayed by today's emotional roller coaster, I confessed to my students, "Yep, we're all drained, literally given out. However, it's about summertime, and most of us have had just about enough of the old three R's—*Readin' Ritin'* and *Rithmetic*. Class, your homework (and mine) over the next couple of months is to practice the other three R's, *Rest, Reflect,* and *Recharge*. Your work will be checked in the fall."

June 24

Everyone has a Family—or Ought To

"Just keep swimming."

Dory, from Finding Nemo

A few days ago, the school closed for the year, and I'm already missing it. Maybe not so much the cafeteria duty or lesson planning, but the reason for all of it—a bunch of messy, snaggletooth truth-tellers. When I left my room for the summer, it was eerily quiet and antiseptic with a faint hint of *Pine-Sol.* The door with my name on it is now locked. My bulletin boards have been stripped of the colorfully laminated children's names and their work samples. The echoes of my footsteps in the empty halls remind me that this year is done.

I'm now at home doing a little reflecting on what happened in that room this year. I know personally that lots of light bulbs went off on both sides of my desk this past year. I am deeply honored by the trust my students demonstrated in me and floored by their bravery in the things they shared with me, mostly without words. I miss their hugs.

I am *celebrating* the end of school by curling up on my couch with a box of Kleenex and watching our favorite movie *Finding Dory.* To "tell the truff," as Hailey told me several times this year, I'm about as blue as Dory. My break just started, and all I can think about is my kindergarten babies, how small they were when they first started, their squeaky little voices, and how much fun it was to be their teacher. Now they are moving on to other educational experiences. I hope each child will continue the construction project we started— building an education that lasts a lifetime. Along the way, I trust every child, like Dory, will find their way back home to family. I'll leave the porch light on.

Epilogue

*The end of all our exploring / Will be to
arrive where we started / And know
the place for the first time.*

T.S. Elliot

It has been a year since Vanessa opened her classroom door and let us peek inside to see what's going on. We have learned that the old name, schoolhouse, may be the most appropriate description of the place where she and her colleagues worldwide do their hard work. With courage and a sense of humor, Vanessa has shown us how the flawed, imperfect people—the big and the little ones—who gather in this *house* learn basic academic skills. More importantly, she's taught us that reading and writing fundamentals are personal. It's best used in the pursuit of a more considerate, tolerant, and loving human being. Good schools are alive with the chaotic, vibrant activity of human beings becoming better human beings.

This generally untidy process involves unpacking new ideas, reshaping old ones, and discarding those that don't work. Like in our own houses, things don't always go as planned. We mess up. However, these errors are the stuff of some of our most powerful learning experiences. Besides the wonderful stories they generate, the natural by-product of learning is a lot of garbage and waste. Consequently, the school*house* is certainly not a sanitary environment, at least not until recently.

Many things have changed after she closed her 2018-2019 school year diary that became this book. Two major events have driven that change and have forced Americans to rethink how we do school and how we think about it. The vicious Covid-19 virus that began in the early spring of 2020 and swept our nation did not spare our students or teachers. We lost too many of both.

Our attempts to mitigate its spread demanded social distancing, face coverings, and good hand hygiene. These necessary precautions were explicitly designed to put artificial barriers between teachers and students or make the relationship more clinically sterile. Currently, body temperatures are the pass to class. On the first day of this new school year, elementary teachers welcomed students to a new year with masks hiding their smiles. The natural reaction of many five and six-year-olds is crying.

Though laudable, these ambitious objectives and behaviors counter how we have traditionally defined the highly personal, often messy, sometimes chaotic connections between teachers and students. Finding the right path forward will be fraught with direr consequences at every turn. It is no surprise that teachers, students, and parents are seriously struggling with these new realities. God bless them all.

This spring, a second huge societal wave finally broke on a street in a Minneapolis suburb. The untimely death of public-school alumnus George Floyd ignited a nationwide protest against racial injustice. Racism, a second hateful virus, has infected too many across our country, and we are struggling with ways to mitigate its spread.

Mr. Floyd and the men responsible for his death all sat in a kindergarten class like Vanessa's. Not surprisingly, psychologists, sociologists, and poets have drawn lines of causation between what happens early in life and things we choose to do later. The life lessons these men learned—somewhere—may have made a real difference.

In school*houses* across America, there are signs of promise in these early attempts to change how we think about the error-prone human beings in the front of the class and those sitting at desks. These strong appeals to the "angels of our better nature" have the potential to radically alter the course of schools, our communities, and our lives. We all have so much to learn.

Gary L. Riggins

About the Authors

 Vanessa Hardaway was born in beautiful Oakridge, TN. After spending eight years in the Nashville/Athens, TN area, she calls Athens, Tennessee her official home. Vanessa has years-long experience in various areas of childhood education and development. She has served as a childcare counselor for the YMCA, a juvenile probation officer for McMinn County juvenile court, and an elementary school teacher at Calhoun Elementary and Niota Elementary schools.

In her spare time, she enjoys motivational speaking and professional development trainings about teacher burnout and other topics with her team partner, Dr. Renee Highberger. She also loves spending time with friends and family.

Vanessa currently lives in Fayetteville, NC, and is a kindergarten teacher in the Cumberland County School District.

Gary L. Riggins

Gary L Riggins is a Professor of Educational Psychology at Lee University. His first book, *Reflections: The 75-year story of the Church of God Home for Children,* won the 1994 Charles W. Conn Historical Writing Award. The Helen DeVos College of Education's highest award for graduate writing (the Riggins Writing Award) was named in his honor. He is also a past president of the Tennessee Conference of Graduate Schools (2011 to 2012). Gary most recently served as a featured columnist for the *Christian Educators Journal.* He completed his doctoral story studies and Educational Psychology at the University of Tennessee in Knoxville with postgraduate studies at the University of Louisville.